Liberty-Loving Lafayette

How "America's Favorite Fighting Frenchman"
Helped Win Our Independence

ISBN: 978-0-9909408-3-8 (Hardcover)
ISBN: 978-0-9909408-1-4 (Paperback)
ISBN: 978-0-9909408-2-1 (E-book)

Library of Congress Control Number: 2020909037

Cover adapted from *Lafayette's Baptism of Fire* by E. Percy Moran, 1909

All pictures used in this work are in the public domain.

"America's favorite fighting Frenchman"—Hamilton © 2015
by Lin-Manuel Miranda

Publisher: Dorothea Jensen
Contoocook NH

The author welcomes performance videos of this work for posting online.
Please contact: PastTimesPress@gmail.com.

Liberty-Loving Lafayette

How "America's Favorite Fighting Frenchman"
Helped Win Our Independence

by

Dorothea Jensen

Publisher: Dorothea Jensen
Contoocook ,NH
2020

Dedication

To Major General Marie-Joseph Paul Yves Roch Gilbert du Motier de Lafayette, formerly known as the Marquis* de Lafayette,

who was called Gilbert** by his friends,

and whose help was vital in our Revolutionary War

* Lafayette gave up his title during the French Revolution

** pronounced "ZHIL-BARE"

Table of Contents

The Marquis de Lafayette In the Uniform of a Major General
by Charles Willson Peale, 1780
Independence National Historical Park

Liberty-Loving Lafayette

So listen up, my children, and I'll do my best to tell

How a teenaged French aristocrat served all of us so well.[1]

Without his help, we might have lost our fight for Liberty,

And we'd still be lowly subjects of the British monarchy!

WILLIAM HENRY, DUKE OF GLOUCESTER

King George III's Younger Brother
by Thomas Gainsborough, circa 1775
National Army Museum (U.K.)

Young Lafayette had dinner with the British king's bro,

Who told him the Americans were "good to go."

Just as soon as he found out about our fight for Liberty

A flame was set alight inside this starry-eyed marquis.[2]

GEORGE III, KING OF ENGLAND
by Allan Ramsay, 1760
Colonial Williamsburg Foundation

GENERAL SIR HENRY CLINTON
Commander-in-Chief
British Forces in America 1778-1782
by Andrea Soldi, circa 1762-1765
The American Museum in Britain

His risking life and fortune quite so very recklessly

Met strenuous objections from his in-law family.

They sent him off to England so that he would change his mind

Where he met King George and Clinton and was richly wined

and dined.[3]

**BARON DE KALB (CENTER) INTRODUCING
LAFAYETTE (LEFT) TO SILAS DEANE**

Engraving from painting by Alonzo Chappel, 1879

New York Public Library Digital Collections

Gilbert came home with mind unchanged, proceeding purposefully.

He'd bought a ship in secret, and he named it *Victory.*

He met with agent Silas Deane[4], and was delighted when

Deane gave him a commission as a Yankee major gen.[5]

His Excellency GEORGE WASHINGTON, Commander in Chief of the American Armies, Marshal of France &c.

GEORGE WASHINGTON
by unidentified artist, 1783
Copy after John Trumbull
National Portrait Gallery
Smithsonian Institution

**ADRIENNE,
MARQUISE DE LAFAYETTE**
by unknown 18th century artist
Christie's

Lafayette had feelings complicated at this point in life.

Should he go fight with Washington, or stay with doting wife?[6]

But the chance of Glory beckoned (not to mention Liberty),

Compelling him to join our fray from far across the sea.

So when the King of France said he'd be subject to arrest,[7]

He sneaked aboard the *Victory* and headed to the West.

He endured the trip across despite some nasty *mal de mer,*

And learned a bit of English by the time he landed there.[8]

INDEPENDENCE HALL IN PHILADELPHIA

by Ferdinand Richardt, circa 1858-63

White House Collection

When he arrived in Philly, though, despite his famous charms,

Nobody welcomed him with even slightly open arms.

"Oh, not another foreigner, we have more than our share,

And such a young and raw recruit we simply cannot bear!

The gall of Mr. Silas Deane, gun-buying is his task,

But he gives lofty ranks galore to all of those who ask!"[9]

MARIE ANTOINETTE, QUEEN OF FRANCE
by Élisabeth Louise Vigée Le Brun, 1778
Kunsthistoriches Museum

But just in time some letters came from far across the sea

From Deane himself, and Franklin[10], who were stationed in "Paree."

"He is both rich and famous, this Marquis de Lafayette.

His friends are French aristocrats, and Queen M. Antoinette.

Just give him a high rank and let him bask in Glory's glow,

But keep him safe, for heaven's sake (and never let him know).

A dead marquis won't help us gain much-needed French support,

But this lad's service in our cause will wow King Louis' court!"[11]

**WASHINGTON AND LAFAYETTE
AT THE BATTLE OF BRANDYWINE**

by John Vanderlyn, circa 1825

Gilcrease Institute of American History and Art

So they made him major general for these diplomatic ends,

And Lafayette and Washington became the best of friends.[12]

LAFAYETTE'S BAPTISM OF FIRE

by E. Percy Moran, 1909

Library of Congress

But just a few weeks later came the fight at Brandywine,

And no one could make Lafayette avoid the battle line.

For when the Brits outflanked us with a most effective trick, [13]

He sallied forth into the fight and helped out double quick.

He rallied men (who'd panicked and were trying to run away)

To stand and fight, and thus he tried his best to save the day.

LAFAYETTE WOUNDED AT THE BATTLE OF BRANDYWINE

Engraved by Charles Henry Jeens, circa 1778-1880

New York Public Library Digital Collections

But to his disappointment his brave efforts hit a wall

When his leg was penetrated by a British musket ball.[14]

He was taken off to Bethlehem to help his leg wound mend,

While the Brits invaded Philly (occupied it in the end).

GENERAL NATHANAEL GREENE
by Charles Willson Peale, 1783
Independence National Historical Park

Gilbert amazed his doctors with his quick recovery.

He rejoined General Washington, and waited hopefully,

Then found his feats at Brandywine (and dedication keen)

Earned honor and respect from "Fighting Quaker" General Greene.[15]

Greene sent him out to skirmish and to scout the British forces

To see how many men there were, and armaments, and horses.

HESSIAN HUSSARS IN AMERICA
by C. Ziegler After Conrad Gessner, 1799
War History Online

Near Gloucester, in the Jerseys, lurked a Hessian company.[16]

The young marquis attacked them, and achieved a victory.

Greene said he searched for danger, when the facts of this were known,

And Lafayette was given a division of his own.[17]

**WASHINGTON AND LAFAYETTE AT VALLEY FORGE
WINTER OF 1777-8**

Engraving by H. B. Hall after Alonzo Chappel, 1931

National Archives

He went along to Valley Forge, enduring cold and damp,

And worked with Hamilton as the Commander's *aides-de-camp*.

His wit and charm kept spirits up for officers and all,

And he helped reveal to Washington the dread Conway Cabal.[18]

The plotters launched another plan to try and split asunder

Young Lafayette and Washington, but 'twas another blunder.

For when they sent the Frenchman north, with Canada the aim,

It didn't take him long to see the whole idea was lame.[19]

At Albany he learned that troops, supplies, and funds were lacking:

All three were indispensable for powerful attacking.

'Twas clear to Lafayette that this "invasion" plan would fizzle,

So he hastened back to Valley Forge despite the snow and drizzle.

BARON VON STEUBEN AT VALLEY FORGE

by Augustus G. Heaton, 1907

National War College

And when Von Steuben trained the men, the Marquis lent his aid

To turn the rabble into troops upon the Grand Parade.[20]

Then word arrived at Valley Forge that France was our ally,

And a "fire of joy" from every gun was shot into the sky.

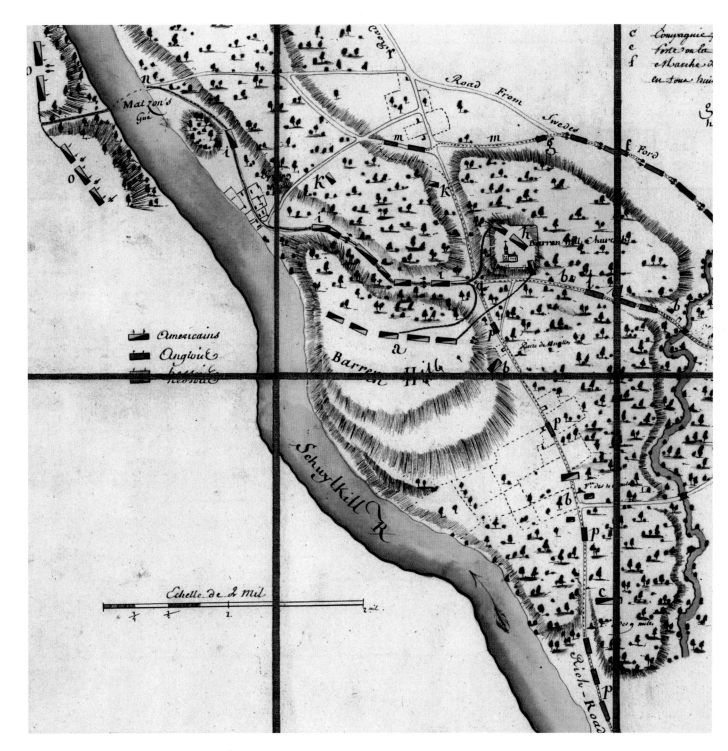

MAP OF THE BATTLE OF BARREN HILL, MAY 20, 1778

by Michel Capitaine du Chesnoy, *Aide-de-Camp* of Lafayette, 1778

Bi-Color Rectangles = Lafayette's Forces (2,200 men)

Solid Rectangles = British and Hessians (16,000 men)

Library of Congress

While British "brass" in Philly partied on in luxury,[21]

George Washington kept fretting what their strategy would be.

So he sent Lafayette in May to see what he could see;

Would Redcoats go to Valley Forge, or back to NYC?[22]

He ended up at Barren Hill, Brit forces all around.

Outnumbered, Lafayette was trapped, until escape was found.

With marching skills drummed into them upon the Grand Parade,

His troops slipped to the river bank where they could safely wade,

And left behind the British, whose commanders had assumed

That "The Boy" would be their captive; when he wasn't, how they

fumed![23]

WASHINGTON RALLYING THE TROOPS AT MONMOUTH

Emanuel Leutze, circa 1851-1854

University of California Berkeley

Then when the Brits left Philly and hightailed it out of town,

It wasn't until Monmouth that our forces chased them down.

Brave Lafayette stood ready to command our troops that day.

But General Lee took precedence, so led the battle fray,

Then messed it up completely when he ordered a retreat,

And all thought Lafayette should have been in the driver's seat.[24]

ENTRY OF THE FRENCH SQUADRON IN NEWPORT BAY AUG. 8, 1778

by Pierre Ozanne, 1778

Library of Congress

When finally ships from France arrived to lend us their support,

Their admiral, D'Estaing, was sent to help attack Newport.

But egos came in conflict when the battle was begun,

And the French fleet sailed away before a victory was won.[25]

The marquis was recruited then to act as go-between,

To help smooth ruffled feathers, and make everything serene.

LOUIS XVI, KING OF FRANCE AND NAVARRE

by Antoine-François Callet, 1779

National Portrait Gallery

Smithsonian Institution

This blundering, however, showed we needed something more

To fix up the alliance and ensure we'd win the war.

So Lafayette sailed back to France and hounded king and court

To send more soldiers and more ships to beef up French support.

**JEAN-BAPTISTE-DONATIEN DE VIMEUR
COMTE DE ROCHAMBEAU**

Commander of French Troops in America

by Charles-Philippe Larivière, 1834

National Portrait Gallery

Smithsonian Institution

And in the end, France doubled down against the British foe:

She sent more troops and ships and guns, and also Rochambeau[26].

**_L'HERMIONE_ REPLICA ARRIVING AT YORKTOWN, VIRGINIA
JUNE 2015**

Photo by Dorothea Jensen, 2015

The young marquis sailed back aboard the frigate, *L'Hermione*,

And Boston wildly welcomed him, as if one of its own.[27]

When Lafayette told Washington more help was soon at hand,

The general, delighted, granted him a new command.[28]

BENEDICT ARNOLD IN HIS BRITISH UNIFORM

By Robert Pollard, 1782

National Portrait Gallery

Smithsonian Institution

40

But soon the British headed South, which they deemed "loyalist,"

And thought (mistakenly) all Southerners were "royalist."

The traitor Arnold joined them there, ransacking as he went.

To capture him and hang him high, young Lafayette was sent.[29]

Arnold escaped, but "Our Marquis"[30] achieved a greater goal,

Maneuvered most judiciously, and whacked a bigger "mole."

GENERAL LORD CHARLES CORNWALLIS

British Commander at Yorktown

by Daniel Gardner, circa early 1780s

American Revolution Museum at Yorktown

For he bottled up Cornwallis at Virginia's Town of York,

And then DeGrasse's fleet arrived to place the crucial "cork."[31]

By pinning down the British in the fall of '81,

Gilbert set up the scene for Independence to be won.

SURRENDER OF LORD CORNWALLIS

By John Trumbull, 1820

Rotunda of the United States Capitol

He awaited the arrival of that consummate combo:

The "Father of our Country" and the Frenchman, Rochambeau.[32]

When Washington appeared, with men, materiel, and horses,

He put "The Boy" in charge of nearly one-third of our forces.

Thus on the Yorktown battlefield, our fa-vor-ite marquis

Performed a starring role[33] to win this final vic-to-ry.[34]

**GILBERT MOTIER, THE MARQUIS DE LAFAYETTE
AS A FRENCH LIEUTENANT GENERAL, 1791**

Joseph-Désiré Court, 1834

United States Embassy in France

46

So raise a cheer for Lafayette, who so loved Liberty.

Without him we would not have won our Independency!

Glossary

aide-de-camp—a personal assistant or secretary to a military leader (French), literally "helper of/in the camp"

armaments—military weapons and equipment

blunder—mistake

"(The) Boy"—a nickname some British officers called Lafayette to make fun of him because of his youth

brass—"top brass" is a slang term for high-ranking military officers

cabal—a secret conspiracy

combo—slang for combination

consummate—supreme

division—a large military unit, often composed of several regiments

fray—fight, battle, or skirmish

frigate—a fast and maneuverable warship

Grand Parade—a large open field at Valley Forge upon which Van Steuben and Lafayette and others trained the Continental troops

Independency—an old-fashioned term for independence

(The) Jerseys—at that time, New Jersey was split into two parts, East Jersey and West Jersey, so therefore called "the Jerseys"

judiciously—using good judgment

loyalist—one who remained loyal to the British monarchy

mal de mer—seasickness (French), literally "sickness of the sea" (pronounced *moll de mare*)

maneuver—to move skillfully or carefully

marquis—a middle-ranking nobleman, above a count and below a duke

materiel—military materials and equipment

mole—in the arcade game "whack-a-mole," when a player pounds one "mole" into a hole with a mallet, another pops up from a different hole

NYC—abbreviation for New York City, which the British army occupied from 1776 until 1783

Paree—anglicized spelling of the French pronunciation of "Paris"

Philly—nickname for Philadelphia, seat of the American government during the Revolution

precedence—given priority because of importance, order, rank, or seniority

rally—to urge troops to reassemble and continue fighting

ransack—to raid and destroy

royalist—a supporter of the king

sally forth—a movement of a military unit, usually coming out from a stronghold

Acknowledgement

Many thanks to Alan Hoffman, President of the American Friends of Lafayette, and translator of *Lafayette in America in 1824 and 1825: Journal of a Voyage to the United States,* for helping me make the history in Liberty-Loving Lafayette as accurate as possible. (Any remaining errors are my own.)

Selected Bibliography

Castrovilla, Selene. *Revolutionary Friends: General George Washington and the Marquis de Lafayette.* Honesdale, PA: Calkins Creek, 2013.

Gaines, James R. *For Liberty and Glory: Washington, Lafayette, and Their Revolutions.* New York City: W. W. Norton & Company, 2007

Kramer, LLoyd. *Lafayette in Two Worlds,: Public Cultures and Personal Identities in an Age of Revolutions.* Chapel Hill: University of North Carolina Press,1999.

Unger, Harlow Giles. *Lafayette.* Hoboken, NJ: Wiley, 2003

Vowell, Sarah. *Lafayette in the Somewhat United States.* New York City: Riverhead Books, 2016

A Buss from Lafayette

**AUTHOR DOROTHEA JENSEN RECEIVES
A "BUSS" FROM LAFAYETTE (BEN GOLDMAN).**

Photo by Julien Icher, Founder of The Lafayette Trail, 2018

About the Author

DOROTHEA JENSEN
Photo by Hank Parfitt, 2017

Dorothea Jensen is a former teacher who has lived all over the United States, as well as in Holland and Brazil. New Hampshire has been her home since 1991. She earned a BA in English at Carleton College and an MA in Secondary Education at the University of New Mexico.

Dorothea has been writing historical fiction for many years. Her first novel about the American Revolution, *The Riddle of Penncroft Farm,* has been in print since 1989. A Teachers' Choices selection of the then International Reading Association, it is used in schools around the country. Her second historical novel, *A Buss from Lafayette,* released in 2016, centers on a clever but troubled 14-year-old girl, Clara, whose life is profoundly changed by meeting General Lafayette during his 1824-5 Farewell Tour. During the course of the story, Clara learns all about what the young Marquis de Lafayette did to help us win the American Revolution. Dorothea also co-authored *A Buss from Lafayette Teacher's Guide* for classroom and homeschool use.

In addition, she writes award-winning modern Christmas stories, the Izzy Elf Series, in verse (for kids aged 6+) about Santa's twenty-first century, high-tech elves: Bizzy, Blizzy, Dizzy, Fizzy, Frizzy, Quizzy, Tizzy, and Whizzy.

Combining her passion for history with her delight in composing rhymes, Dorothea started finding couplets forming in her head about Lafayette. Inspired by the musical Hamilton and by Longfellow's poem, "The Midnight Ride of Paul Revere," (which she had to memorize in the fifth grade) she ended up writing this rhyming history of Lafayette's key role in our Revolution.

Praise for This Work

"An ode to the great Lafayette, beautifully told and richly illustrated"
—*Alan R. Hoffman, Translator,* Lafayette in America in 1824 and 1825: Journal of a Voyage to the United States, *and President, The American Friends of Lafayette*

"A great addition to the [Lafayette] canon"—*Diane Shaw, Director Emerita of Special Collections & College Archives, Lafayette College*

"Dorothea Jensen brings Lafayette to life for all ages"—*Chuck Schwam, Publisher,* American Friends of Lafayette Gazette

Other Works

A Buss From Lafayette

A playful kiss from a world-famous Revolutionary War hero in 1825 changes a spirited young girl's life forever in this award-winning MG/YA historical novel.

"A winning historical tale that may appeal to young fans of the musical *Hamilton*".
—*Kirkus Reviews*

"Jensen makes Lafayette come alive in a way [readers] will remember. Historical accuracy, character development, and engaging dialogue enliven this narrative and make it an enjoyable read."
—*Booklife Prize in Fiction*

A Buss From Lafayette Teacher's Guide

This is a complete guide (with answer key) for using A Buss from Lafayette for the schoolroom. Main topics include Lafayette's vital role in the Revolution, his 1824-5 Farewell Tour, and everyday life and customs in 1820s America.

"The need for teachers to find ways to make history interesting is crucial. *A Buss from Lafayette* will provide not only historic background of the revolutionary time . . . but also a story that all children can identify with . . . [This] guide also gives many wonderful suggestions of how to integrate subjects with the historical content of this novel [and] suggests questions that challenge higher level thinking.
—*Susan Elliott, Ph.D.*

The Riddle of Penncroft Farm

Young Lars Olafson reluctantly moves from Minnesota to an old family farm near Valley Forge. He finally makes a friend, whose stories of the American Revolution are those of an eye witness. Will they help Lars solve a mystery?

"Not only is the history presented in an interesting and painless manner, but also readers should come away eager to read more about this period."
—*School Library Journal*

The Santa's Izzy Elves Series

These rhyming, illustrated stories (for kids 5+), modeled after "A Visit from Saint Nicholas," are about eight twenty-first century elves who are technology savvy.

"The author propels her present day take on the classic Christmas poem with gentle humor and suspense, smoothly incorporating lines from the original poem into her lively tale . . ."
—*Kirkus Reviews*

". . .a highly original and wonderfully developed children's book. . .a creative and engaging story."
—*Red City Review*

Social Media Links

Blog

www.dorotheajensen.blogspot.com

Bublish

www.bublish.com/author/view/5755

E-Mail

jensendorothea@gmail.com

Facebook

www.facebook.com/dorothea.jensen.12

Pinterest

www.pinterest.com/dgjensen116

Timelines

abussfromlafayette.com/Timeline Lafayette in the American Revolution

friendsoflafayette.wildapricot.org/Timeline Complete Lafayette Timeline

Twitter

twitter.com/dgjensen116

Vimeo Channel

vimeo.com/dorotheagjensen

Websites

www.abussfromlafayette.com, and www.dorotheajensen.com

YouTube Channel

www.youtube.com   (Search for Dorothea Jensen)

End Notes

1 Marie-Joseph Paul Yves Roch Gilbert du Motier de Lafayette was only nineteen when he first arrived in America in 1777. A marquis, which is a middling aristocratic rank, his family inheritance made him one of the richest men in France. This portrait was painted by Charles Willson Peale at the request of Lafayette's friend, General Washington, before the young Frenchman left for France in January 1779, to seek more aid for America.

2 On August 8, 1775, Lafayette had dinner in Metz, France, with William Henry, Duke of Gloucester, the younger brother of George III, King of England. Gloucester disagreed with his older brother on his treatment of the American colonies (and many other things). Lafayette later said that hearing about the colonists' rebellion on this occasion "enlisted his heart" in the American cause.

3 In an effort to change Lafayette's mind about helping America in its fight for independence, his rich and powerful father-in-law, the Duc d'Ayen, sent him to visit England. As the Duc's uncle was the French ambassador in London, Lafayette's participation in the American war could cause personal and political embarrassment for the family. At any rate, while there, the young marquis was presented to King George III himself. He also went to the opera with General Henry Clinton, later the commander-in-chief of all British forces in America (from 1778 until 1782). (Lafayette was also the guest of honor at a ball given by Lord George Germain, British Secretary for the Colonies.)

4 Silas Deane was an American agent for the Continental Congress in Paris seeking aid from France. Sent to recruit military engineers, he ended up recruiting many experienced (and some inexperienced) officers to join the Continental Army.

5 The rank of major general, which Deane promised to Lafayette, was the highest of any in the Continental army except for that of General George Washington. Although Lafayette had had military training, he had no battle experience at all. This lofty rank, even without troops to command, would have been completely unattainable under normal circumstances.

6 Gilbert married the 14-year-old Adrienne de Noailles, daughter of the Duc D'Ayen, when he was only 16. Although this was an arranged marriage, Gilbert and Adrienne became a devoted couple.

7 King Louis issued an arrest warrant to stop Lafayette from leaving for America. The French government feared having a "celebrity" like Lafayette join the fight on the side of the Americans. This might bring secret ongoing French support for the Americans into the open, and alert the British as to what was going on. (Actually, the British already knew about all this.)

8 Baron de Kalb, a Prussian officer who had fought in the French army, had been to America previously as a French agent to assess how committed the Patriots were to the cause of independence. He taught Lafayette some English during their voyage to America on the *Victory*. The two men became good friends.

54

9 A number of unqualified European soldiers received promises of high rank in the Continental Army from American agent Silas Deane. Some arrogantly demanded exorbitant pay when they arrived in America. Many of these men were not accepted by Congress and went back to Europe.

10 Ben Franklin, America's "minister" (ambassador) to France, had the challenging task of trying to persuade an absolute monarchy to support a rebellion against another monarch —that of its old enemy, England. Ironically, this support of America, payback for the Seven Years' War (French and Indian War), nearly bankrupted France. This turned out to be a contributing factor for the later revolt against its own king.

11 Deane and Franklin did write letters stating these views (with slightly different wording).

12 The extremely close friendship between the fatherless Lafayette and the childless Washington is evidenced by numerous accounts and letters.

13 On September 11, 1777, at Brandywine Creek in Pennsylvania, Washington tried to block the British from capturing Philadelphia, the American capital at that time. British General Howe sent part of his army towards Chadd's Ford, where Washington was waiting, as a diversion. The main British forces marched north, however, crossed the Brandywine north of where it forked (at fords unknown to Washington), and came down behind the untrained Patriot forces. Although Lafayette had no one officially under his command, his courageous rallying of the troops who were on the battlefield was remarkable for his first time under fire. Later he also set up a control point to keep the retreat of American troops from turning into a rout.

14 This leg wound, suffered by Lafayette at Brandywine in his first ever battle, compelled him to leave the army to recover with the Moravians in Bethlehem, Pennsylvania. Lafayette wrote this to his wife: "the English honoured me with a musket ball, which slightly wounded me in the leg."

15 Nathanael Greene was expelled by the pacifist Quakers because of his military career. He briefly served as Quartermaster General of the Continental Army, but ended up becoming the commander of the southern campaign. He was exceptionally able and a good friend of Washington's.

16 The Hessians were troops.George III "rented" from the rulers of Hesse-Cassel and other German states. Approximately 30,000 Hessians fought on the British side during the Revolution. Something like 5,000 of these Germans stayed on after the war.

17 Lafayette was still a major general without any men under his command until General Greene sent him to lead a small number of troops on an independent foray near Gloucester, New Jersey. Afterwards, Greene wrote to Washington: "The marquis is determined to be in the way of danger." Such courage and effective leadership earned him the command of an entire division.

[18] Lafayette's charm and wit may well have helped alleviate the gloom at Valley Forge headquarters. While there, the young marquis wrote a passionate letter confirming to Washington that the Irishman Thomas Conway (appointed quartermaster at Valley Forge over Washington's vehement protests) and others were plotting to replace Washington as commander-in-chief with General Gates, the so-called hero of Saratoga. This secret plot was called the "Conway Cabal."

[19] Over Washington's strong objections, Congress set up a "Board of War" to supervise his conduct of the war, and Gates, his bitter rival, was elected president of it. One of the goals of the "cabalists" on the Board was to separate Lafayette from Washington, for which purpose they ordered the young Frenchman to lead an attack on Canada. They did not, however, provide Lafayette with sufficient troops, funds, or supplies to accomplish this. The only good outcome of this fizzled project was that Lafayette was able to talk forty-seven Oneida warriors into fighting on the American side.

[20] The Prussian officer Baron Von Steuben worked with the American troops at Valley Forge on the large field called the Grand Parade by training men who then trained others and so forth. By the end of the winter, this "School of the Soldier" had transformed the Patriots into an effective fighting force. Following Von Steuben's methods, while at Valley Forge Lafayette trained the men under his own command.

[21] The British "Top Brass," General Howe and other British officers, partied all winter in Philadelphia. (The Loyalist young ladies who enthusiastically flirted with the Redcoats during the British Occupation were said to have come down with "Scarlet Fever.") Just before Barren Hill, a huge farewell party for Howe even featured "joisting" knights.

[22] New York City (NYC) was held by the British for most of the war so was the center of their American operations. Washington worried that Howe's army occupying Philadelphia might attack Valley Forge rather than re-joining the rest of the army in New York. He sent Lafayette to scout out what the British were planning to do.

[23] Because of his men's training at Valley Forge, Lafayette was able to maneuver them away from the British trap at Barren Hill and cross the Schuylkill River at Matson's Ford. British General Howe had boasted that he would capture Lafayette— whom some British officers called "The Boy"— and would bring him to dinner in Philadelphia as his guest that evening.

[24] Lafayette was originally supposed to lead this attack. Once it was decided that a larger force would be sent after the British, however, General Lee insisted he should be in command because of his "seniority." Lee then prematurely ordered a retreat, which infuriated Washington. Lafayette, on the other hand, distinguished himself at this battle. (After this, Lee was courtmartialed and never served in the Continental army again.)

[25] French Admiral D'Estaing later said he departed in order to attack a British fleet, but a storm intervened. John Sullivan, the American commander trying to recapture Newport from the British, wrote angry letters. In them he complained about D'Estaing leaving the Americans to fight and lose the rest of the battle alone. Washington finally had to caution Sullivan to pipe down. (Lafayette led a division in this battle, by the way.)

26 General Rochambeau commanded the French troops who fought in America from 1780 on. They accompanied Washington and the Continentals on the long trek from New York to Yorktown, where they helped win the final major battle of the war.

27 Lafayette received a tumultuous welcome in Boston when he arrived there on April 28, 1780, on the French frigate *L'Hermione* (pronounced lair-me-own in French). The ship was named *Hermione* (the feminine version of the name, as ships are considered to be female) after Hermes, the Greek messenger god. This was quite appropriate, as Lafayette was bearing a secret message of significant additional French support. Obviously, modern French and American flags were flying on the replica ship in 2015. The Bourbon flag (white background with gold fleurs-de-lis) would have been flown on the original ship.

28 Washington gave Lafayette command of some light infantry. When the British decided to take the war to the "Loyalist" South, Washington sent Lafayette and 1200 men (many from his light infantry troops) to Virginia. His assignment was to capture and execute the traitor Benedict Arnold, who, as a British general, was laying waste to the Commander's home colony.

29 Lafayette himself said, "As a result of [Arnold's] treason and desertion, I was to deliver justice swiftly and without delay!"

30 The Continental troops affectionately called Lafayette "Our Marquis."

31 The French fleet commanded by Admiral DeGrasse had been in the West Indies, but arrived in Chesapeake Bay just in time to defeat a British fleet there. By thus gaining control of the mouth of the bay, DeGrasse's fleet was able to blockade Lord Cornwallis and his army in Yorktown.

32 French Admiral DeGrasse urged Lafayette to launch an immediate assault on Yorktown because his own and Lafayette's troops would have been sufficient to do this. Lafayette, however, insisted that they wait for Washington, whom he felt deserved the credit of any possible major victory.

33 Lafayette's division was given the position of honor on the right flank of the American front line. His good friends, Hamilton and Laurens, who led the crucial attack on Redoubt #10, were under his command.

34 Lord Cornwallis, the British general at Yorktown, is not actually in the Trumbull painting of the surrender (despite the title) because he was not present at the ceremony. Claiming he was too sick to attend, Cornwallis sent his subordinate, General O'Hara, in his place. As per military protocol, O'Hara presented Cornwallis' sword to Washington's subordinate, General Lincoln. This deprived the "Father of Our Country" of the honor of personally accepting the sword from the actual commander he'd defeated in this final major battle of the American Revolution. He did, however, have the no doubt immense pleasure of watching nearly 8,000 British troops lay down their arms.

Made in the USA
Las Vegas, NV
17 November 2020